LILY & HODGE
& DR JOHNSON

CAT. *n. f.* [*katz*,Teuton. *chat*, Fr.] A domeſtick animal that catches mice, commonly reckoned by naturaliſts the loweſt order of the leonine ſpecies.

LEXICO'GRAPHER. *n. f.* [λεξικὸν and γράφω; *lexicographe*, French.] A writer of dictionaries; a harmleſs drudge, that buſies himſelf in tracing the original, and detailing the ſignification of words.

LILY & HODGE
& Dᴿ JOHNSON

Wood engravings by Yvonne Skargon
Words by Samuel Johnson

SILENT BOOKS

This little book is for John who,
too, would fetch oysters

First published in Great Britain 1991
by Silent Books, Swavesey, Cambridge CB4 5RA

© Engravings copyright Yvonne Skargon 1991
© This edition copyright Silent Books 1991

ISBN 1 85183 028 6

Typeset by Goodfellow & Egan
Printed in Great Britain by
St Edmundsbury Press, Bury St Edmunds, Suffolk

*'I shall never forget the indulgence with which he
treated Hodge, his cat; for whom he himself used to go out
and buy oysters, lest the servants having that trouble should
take a dislike of the poor creature.'*

It is safe to assume that no one who does not warm to
Boswell's anecdote will be very interested in this little book.
But those who do may like to know that another of
Dr Johnson's cats was called Lily and that in the hope that
the two kittens that moved in at the end of 1989 might share
the literary predilections of their predecessor Oscar
(of *The Importance of Being Oscar* fame), they were named Lily and Hodge.
So far, as will be apparent, the hope has not been fulfilled.

Indeed, the conjunction of Samuel Johnson LL.D, D.C.L. with
such sprigs of irresponsibility can only be justified by
invoking the Doctor's indulgent response to the young man who
having asked 'Pray, now, what could you give, old gentleman,
to be as young and sprightly as I am?' was told 'Why, Sir,
I think I would almost be content to be as foolish.'

The engravings record episodes in the first eighteen-months
of Hodge and Lily's lives. Like his name-sake, Hodge may
properly be described as 'a very fine cat, a very fine cat indeed'
but Lily no more resembles her eponym in being 'very well behaved'
than she does in being a striped tabby rather than a 'white kitling'.

The words accompanying the engravings are from various of
Johnson's writings, letters and reported speech. The dictionary
definitions together with Johnson's citations from earlier
writers are taken from the sixth edition (1785)
of his *Dictionary of the English Language.*

K I T T E N It is probable that the true
singular is *Kit*, the diminutive of *cat*, of
which the old plural was *kitten*, or *young
cats*, which was in time taken for the
singular, like *chicken*.
A young cat.

I would rather be attacked than unnoticed.

PLAYFUL Sportive: full of levity.
He is scandalized at youth for being lively and
at childhood for being playful.
ADDISON'S *Spectator*

Remember that all tricks are either knavish
or childish

If you are idle, be not solitary . . .

. . . if you are solitary be not idle.

It is by studying little things that we attain
the great art of having as little misery and
as much happiness as possible.

To T E A S E To torment with
importunity, to vex with assiduous
impertinence.

TRANQUILLITY Quiet; peace of
mind; peace of condition; freedom from
perturbation.
You can scarce imagine any hero passing from
one stage of life to another with so much
tranquillity, so easy a transition, and so
laudable a behaviour. POPE

I look upon it, that he who does not mind
his belly will hardly mind anything else.

The endearing elegance of female
friendship.

A B L U T I O N The act of cleaning, or
washing clean.
    There is a natural analogy between the ablution
of the body and the purification of the soul . . .
T A Y L O R

S O M N O L E N C Y Sleepiness;
   inclination to sleep.

To A W A K E   To break from sleep; to
cease to sleep.

Alack, I am afraid they have awak'd.

S H A K E S P E A R E

AMBUSHMENT Ambush;
surprise: a word now not used.

Like as a wily fox, that having spied
Where on a sunny bank the lambs do play
Full closely creeping by the hinder side,
Lies in ambushment of his hoped prey.

SPENSER

H I D E and S E E K A play in which
   some hide themselves and another seeks
   them.
   The boys and girls would venture to come and
   play hide and seek in my hair.
                                        Gulliver's Travels

C O Q U E T T E A gay, airy girl; a girl
who endeavours to attract notice.
A coquette and a tinder box are sparkled.
ARBUTHNOT AND POPE

We would all be idle if we could.

To SWINGLE
1 To dangle
2 To swing in pleasure

To B I R D To catch birds.

I do invite you tomorrow morning to my house,
to breakfast, after we'll a birding together.

SHAKESPEARE

He washed himself with oriental
scrupulosity.

A generous and elevated mind is
distinguished by nothing more certainly
than an eminent degree of curiosity.

Fie! Fie! my dears, no sparring: off with
your mufflers, and fight it fairly out.

That is the happiest conversation where
there is no competition, no vanity, but a
calm, quiet interchange of sentiments.

All intellectual improvement arises from leisure.

AFTERWORD

Samuel Johnson was born at Lichfield, Staffordshire
on 18 September 1709, the son of a bookseller.
Educated at Lichfield Grammar School and Pembroke College, Oxford
he moved to London in 1737 where he established himself as
the archetypal Londoner and the pre-eminent
literary figure of his time.
His *Dictionary of the English Language* was published in 1775.
Ten years later he received the degree of LL.D from Trinity College,
Dublin and in 1775 was made D.C.L. by Oxford University.
He died in London on 13 December 1784
and is buried in Westminster Abbey.

Lily and Hodge were born in a barn in Suffolk 280 years
to the day after Samuel Johnson. Deserted by their mother
when 6 weeks old they were rescued by Bury Stray Cats
and raised by hand at the vets. From the age of 3 months
they have set about overcoming their inauspicious beginnings
by taking over the time, attention, affections and home
of Yvonne Skargon whose wood-engravings record the
first eighteen months of a new and demanding enchantment.